I0805228

IMPACTING EARTH
HOW PEOPLE CHANGE THE LAND

OPERATING FARMS AND LOGGING COMPANIES

JASON BRAINARD

PowerKiDS press
New York

Published in 2019 by The Rosen Publishing Group, Inc.
29 East 21st Street, New York, NY 10010

Copyright © 2019 by The Rosen Publishing Group, Inc.

All rights reserved. No part of this book may be reproduced in any form without permission in writing from the publisher, except by a reviewer.

First Edition

Editor: Jennifer Lombardo
Book Design: Tanya Dellaccio

Photo Credits: Cover Tim Graham/Getty Images News/Getty Images; p. 5 Klanarong Chitmung/Shutterstock.com; p. 7 Dan Thornberg/Shutterstock.com; p. 9 lowsun/Shutterstock.com; p. 10 Fotokostic/Shutterstock.com; p. 11 Kletr/Shutterstock.com; p. 13 (main) Syda Productions/Shutterstock.com; p. 13 (inset) STR/AFP/Getty Images; p. 15 (main) mogilami/Shutterstock.com; p. 15 (inset) Apple's Eyes Studio/Shutterstock.com; p. 17 Erik Monge/Shutterstock.com; p. 18 ufokim/Shutterstock.com; p. 19 Imagenet/Shutterstock.com; p. 20 tchara/Shutterstock.com; p. 21 Henry Arden/Cultura/Getty Images; p. 22 Steve Heap/Shutterstock.com.

Library of Congress Cataloging-in-Publication Data

Names: Brainard, Jason, author.
Title: Operating farms and logging companies / Jason Brainard.
Description: New York : PowerKids Press, [2019] | Series: Impacting Earth: how people change the land | Includes index.
Identifiers: LCCN 2018032894| ISBN 9781538341988 (library bound) | ISBN 9781538341964 (pbk.) | ISBN 9781538341971 (6 pack)
Subjects: LCSH: Agriculture–Environmental aspects–Juvenile literature. | Farm management–Environmental aspects–Juvenile literature. | Forests and forestry–Environmental aspects–Juvenile literature. | Logging–Environmental aspects–Juvenile literature. | Nature–Effect of human beings on–Juvenile literature.
Classification: LCC S519 .B78 2019 | DDC 630-dc23
LC record available at https://lccn.loc.gov/2018032894

Manufactured in the United States of America

CPSIA Compliance Information: Batch #CWPK19. For Further Information contact Rosen Publishing, New York, New York at 1-800-237-9932

CONTENTS

HOMES AND FOOD

People once hunted for meat and picked all the plants they ate. They made tools to cut down trees they could burn to heat their homes. Today, most of our food comes from farms. People don't use wood for heating as much, but we use it for other things. Most people don't need to cut down trees to get wood. Instead, logging companies cut down trees and sell the wood. This has greatly changed the way Earth's land looks.

SHEEP!

Sheep are raised on farms for their meat and their wool. This wool is cut off and turned into yarn to make clothes and blankets.

A FARM

Some people grow crops and raise animals on farms. There are many kinds of farms. Milk comes from cows on dairy farms. Just about every fruit or vegetable you can think of is grown on a farm somewhere. The plants we use to make clothes, such as cotton, are grown on farms. To make a farm, people have to change the land by clearing a large space where plants and animals can live and grow.

FERTILIZER

Animal and plant waste is used to **fertilize** soil. This helps crops grow better.

THE FOREST

Large areas of trees are called forests. Most of the wood we use comes from forests full of trees planted by logging companies, which cut down the trees when they're grown. The trees are then taken away to be **processed**. After it's processed, the wood is cut into smaller pieces so it's ready for people to use. Because they're both planting and cutting down trees, logging companies change the land in two ways.

TOOLS OF THE TRADE

People use many tools on farms and logging sites. There can be danger! Large trucks and tractors zip around. **Chemicals** used to kill weeds can make animals and people sick. Chemicals can also change the land by killing other plants if the chemicals aren't gotten rid of properly. The tools used to cut trees and **harvest** crops can be big and sharp.

FARMERS AND LOGGERS

There are many jobs in farming and logging. Both fields use **scientists** to look at how healthy the soil is. Some people's jobs are to make sure that other workers are safe. Trucks and tractors need drivers. Animals need to be fed. Barns need to be cleaned. Fruit needs to be picked. Trees need to be cut down.

APRIL 10, 1872

About 1 million trees were planted on this day, which was the first Arbor Day. Every year, people plant more trees on Arbor Day.

PROCESSING

After loggers cut down trees, the logs are taken to mills. A mill is a place where workers use machines to cut the logs into smaller pieces. People buy these pieces of wood to build things like houses and furniture. Farmed goods, such as meat and produce, must be cleaned and packed before they're sold. Processing logs and food requires factories and power plants. These places create a lot of pollution.

WHAT WE DON'T WANT

Farming and logging can change the land and make fresh water dirty. They may ruin the **habitats** of wild animals. Some businesses use **poison** to kill weeds and pests. Trucks and tractors may spill gas. Animal waste from farms stinks. This all needs to be cleaned up if another type of business wants to use the land later on.

DEFORESTATION

Deforestation is the act or result of cutting down or burning all the trees in an area. If we do this too much, there won´t be enough trees.

HELPING THE LAND

People who own and work for farms and logging companies need to take care of the land, or the land won't be able to produce more plants or **support** animals. Planting new trees makes sure there will be new forests. Keeping the water clean helps plants, animals, and people.

IS IT WORTH IT?

Are farming and logging worth all the work and the changes to the land? If we didn't have farms, we wouldn't have many things. We wouldn't have stores filled with fruits and vegetables. We wouldn't have hamburgers and pizza. And without logging, where would the wood to build a house or chair come from?

PESTICIDES

Most farms spray their crops with pesticides, which are poisons that kill bugs. Give an apple or any other fruit or vegetable a good wash before eating it.

KEEPING IT GOING

The land changes when we log and farm. We must take care of the land and clean up the messes we make when we use **resources**. Modern farming can give us a steady supply of food. Logging gives us wood to build the houses we live in. But the land will only take care of us if we take care of it.

GLOSSARY

chemical: Matter that can be mixed with other matter to cause changes.

fertilize: To add something to the soil to help plants grow.

habitat: The natural home for plants, animals, and other living things.

harvest: To gather crops after they've grown.

poison: A matter that can hurt or kill living things.

process: Actions that change something, or to change to be more useful to people.

resource: Something that can be used.

scientist: Someone who studies a science.

support: To give what is needed.

INDEX

WEBSITES

Due to the changing nature of Internet links, PowerKids Press has developed an online list of websites related to the subject of this book. This site is updated regularly. Please use this link to access the list:
www.powerkidslinks.com/hpcl/farms